A U.S. INDEPENDENCE
TIME CAPSULE

ARTIFACTS OF THE NATION'S BEGINNINGS

by Natalie Fowler

Consultant:
Richard Bell, PhD
Associate Professor of History
University of Maryland, College Park

CAPSTONE PRESS
a capstone imprint

T0050820

Capstone Captivate is published by Capstone Press, an imprint of Capstone.
1710 Roe Crest Drive
North Mankato, Minnesota 56003
www.capstonepub.com

Library of Congress Cataloging-in-Publication Data is available on the Library of Congress website.
ISBN: 978-1-5435-9230-6 (library binding)
ISBN: 978-1-4966-6628-4 (paperback)
ISBN: 978-1-5435-9237-5 (eBook pdf)

Summary: If the founding fathers and mothers of the United States had built a time capsule to tell the story of the nation's beginnings, what artifacts would be packed inside? Examine a lantern, yellowed documents, and more to learn the story of the colonists' fight for independence.

Photo Credits
Alamy: The History Collection, 20; Architect of the Capitol: 5, 28, 39; DVIC: NARA, 22; Getty Images: The Boston Globe/David L. Ryan, 14, De Agostini Picture Library, 31; iStockphoto: Nastasic, 15; Library of Congress: 17, 37; The Metropolitan Museum of Art: Gift of John Steward Kennedy, 1897, 26; National Archives and Records Administration: cover (top right), 25, 30, 34, 38, 41; North Wind Picture Archives: 8, 10, 16; Shutterstock: ale-kup (background), cover and throughout, David Smart, cover (left), 36, EQRoy, 6, L F File, 32, PhotoItaliaStudio, 18, Songquan Deng, cover (middle), Tupungato, 42, W. Scott McGill, 27, Yuriy Boyko, 23; Valley Forge National Historical Park: The George C. Neumann Collection, 12; XNR Productions: 9

Editorial Credits
Editor: Julie Gassman; Designer: Lori Bye; Media Researcher: Svetlana Zhurkin; Production Specialist: Tori Abraham

All internet sites appearing in back matter were available and accurate when this book was sent to press.

Table of Contents

Words in **bold** are in the glossary.

CHAPTER 1
INTRODUCTION

When something important happens, we want to remember it. One of the ways we can do that is to keep special things from that event. Those things can be evidence that helps to prove what happened, shows us how people reacted, and reminds us what was important about that moment in time. This collection of items could even be saved in a time capsule—a container of artifacts buried away for discovery in the future.

What if there was a special time capsule for each important moment in history? What if you found that time capsule? What would be in it?

In the 1600s and the 1700s, Europeans explored and immigrated to the New World and **colonized** territories. Great Britain, France, the Netherlands, and Spain all had territories in what is now known as the United States.

Thirteen of these territories, or colonies, were under the control of Great Britain and ruled by King George III. These colonies grew more independent, and eventually, the colonists were willing to fight for their freedom. Ultimately, a new nation was born. The story of this new nation—the United States of America—deserves to have its own time capsule.

The first draft of the Declaration of Independence was presented to the Second Continental Congress on June 28, 1776.

CHAPTER 2

THE COLONIZATION OF AMERICA

From the Time Capsule:
REDCOAT

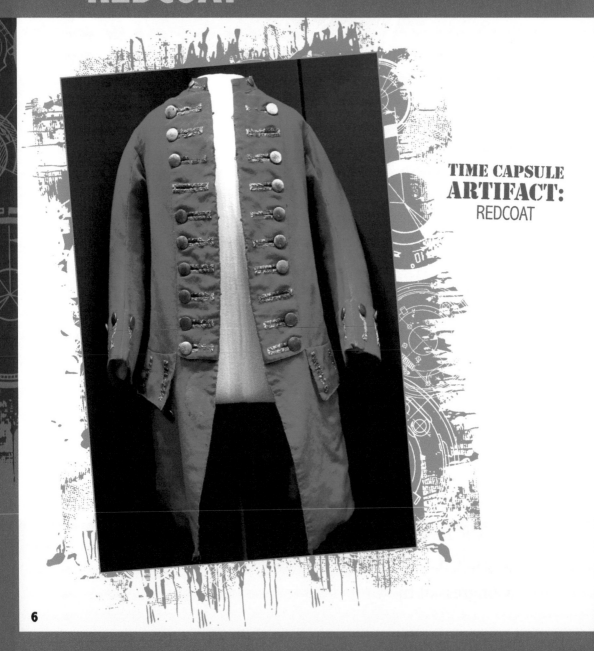

TIME CAPSULE
ARTIFACT:
REDCOAT

As you reach into our time capsule, the first item you might see is clothing. The bright red fabric catches your eye. The gold trim and buttons make it fancy. This coat was actually part of a British soldier's uniform. The British soldiers were called "Redcoats" because of their red uniform.

In the early days of the colonies, there was a need for soldiers in the New World. Both Britain and France claimed the right to rule the same territory between the Appalachian Mountains and along the Mississippi River. Both built forts and established trading posts in the region.

American Indians and the Colonists

American Indians from the Odawa, Iroquois, and Ojibwe nations also lived and hunted in the territory that Britain and France battled over. In the beginning, some of the Native peoples worked with the British and French. They traded goods such as fur pelts in exchange for knives, firearms, fishing hooks, and cooking utensils. However, as the colonies grew, their way of life was disrupted and changed forever.

A war broke out in Europe between France and Great Britain (the Seven Years' War) and in the Americas (the French and Indian War). Some American Indian nations sided with the British. Others favored the French. After years of fighting, both sides agreed to peace and signed a **treaty**. Britain gained most of the control in North America. By 1763, the fighting had ended in the 13 colonies.

Some battles of the French and Indian War were fought in Canada.

The Proclamation of 1763 set a boundary to separate the British colonies from land belonging to American Indian nations. It was supposed to stop the colonies from going west of the Appalachian Mountains.

Even though the war was over, British soldiers remained in the area. The soldiers had an important job—to keep the colonists safe—but it wouldn't be long before they had another reason to stay in the 13 colonies.

RISING TENSIONS

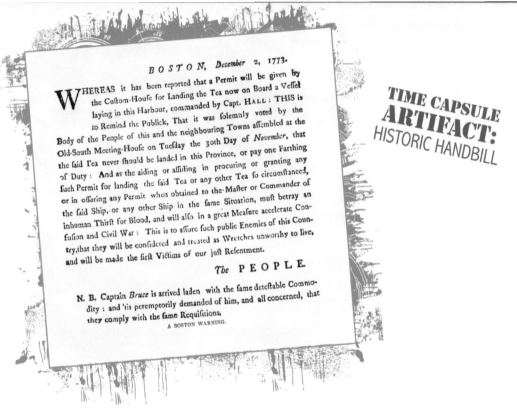

BOSTON, *December* 2, 1773.

WHEREAS it has been reported that a Permit will be given by the Custom-House for Landing the Tea now on Board a Vessel laying in this Harbour, commanded by Capt. HALL: THIS is to Remind the Publick, That it was solemnly voted by the Body of the People of this and the neighbouring Towns assembled at the Old-South Meeting-House on Tuesday the 30th Day of *November*, that the said Tea never should be landed in this Province, or pay one Farthing of Duty: And as the aiding or assisting in procuring or granting any such Permit for landing the said Tea or any other Tea so circumstanced, or in offering any Permit when obtained to the-Master or Commander of the said Ship, or any other Ship in the same Situation, must betray an inhuman Thirst for Blood, and will also in a great Measure accelerate Confusion and Civil War: This is to assure such public Enemies of this Country, that they will be confidered and treated as Wretches unworthy to live, and will be made the first Victims of our just Resentment.

The PEOPLE.

N. B. Captain *Bruce* is arrived laden with the same detestable Commodity: and 'tis peremptorily demanded of him, and all concerned, that they comply with the same Requisitions.

A BOSTON WARNING.

TIME CAPSULE ARTIFACT: HISTORIC HANDBILL

Underneath the soldier's uniform, there may be an old piece of paper dated December 2, 1773. This **handbill** was an announcement that was passed around to the colonists. It reminded them about the Tea Act of 1773.

The wars in Europe and North America had been expensive, and the British government needed money. One of the ways it chose to raise money was to increase taxes. In 1764, the British Parliament began passing laws and creating new taxes for the colonists. Over the next several years, lots of new taxes were imposed on the colonists. They grew angry at this taxation without representation.

Taxation Without Representation

- The Sugar Act of 1764 added taxes to sugar, molasses, wine, cloth, and coffee.

- The Quartering Act of 1765 required colonists to provide housing for British soldiers.

- The Stamp Act of 1765 taxed every printed piece of paper, including legal documents, contracts, newspapers, and even playing cards.

- The Townshend Acts of 1767 required the colonists to pay taxes on glass, lead, paint, paper, and tea.

- The Tea Act of 1773 allowed tea from the East India Company to be sold directly to colonists by British agents, bypassing local merchants.

TIME CAPSULE
ARTIFACT:
MUSKET

You might have to be careful with our next time capsule item. It is an original musket from the Revolutionary War. If you were to pull it out, you would handle the long, skinny gun with care.

It was dangerous to write or speak out against the British government. The colonists began collecting and hiding military supplies like muskets. Without muskets, the colonists would not have any way to fight back against the British Army.

The **patriots** couldn't risk the British soldiers finding their weapons and taking them away. One of the places they hid a great deal of weapons was in the town of Concord, Massachusetts.

In addition to stockpiling supplies, secret groups began to form. The Sons of Liberty organized both peaceful and **extremist** protests against Great Britain. The Daughters of Liberty organized **boycotts** of British products.

Fact

Not everyone in the colonies opposed British rule. One-third of Americans were **loyalists**. They supported King George III and his rule over the colonies.

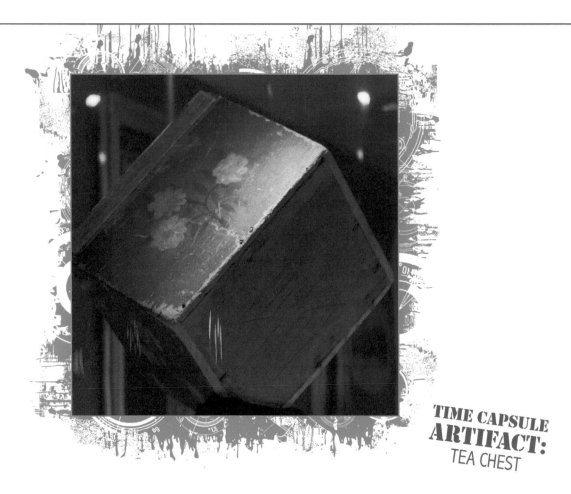

If you were to reach into our time capsule again,
the next item might look a little boring. It's just an old
wooden crate . . . or is it? It is actually an extremely
important piece of history because it is one of the only
surviving crates of tea from the Boston Tea Party.

On November 28, 1773, the first of three ships from the East India Company sailed into the Boston **port** full of tea. The other two ships arrived within a few weeks. The Sons of Liberty were determined that the tea tax would not be paid and the tea would not be unloaded from any of the ships.

In the dark of night, they emptied every chest of tea on board all three ships—342 in all—into the harbor in less than four hours.

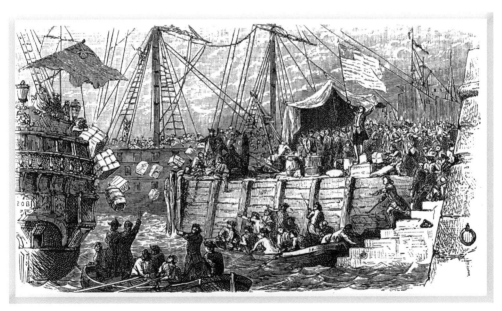

The tea dumped into the harbor was worth about £10,000. Today, it would be worth around $1.7 million.

The Intolerable Acts

Several acts were passed in 1774 to punish the colonists in Massachusetts for the Boston Tea Party. Parliament called these acts the Coercive Acts. The colonists called these acts the Intolerable Acts.

One of these new laws was the Boston Port Act. Parliament declared that the Boston port had to stay closed until Massachusetts paid for the destroyed tea. The port was important to the businesses and colonists in Boston. With it closed, everyone suffered. No one could get the goods they needed—to sell or to buy.

British soldiers took control of Boston harbor in 1768, but the Intolerable Acts took even more rights away from the colonists.

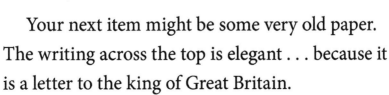

TIME CAPSULE
ARTIFACT:
PETITION TO THE KING

Your next item might be some very old paper.
The writing across the top is elegant . . . because it
is a letter to the king of Great Britain.

Today, Carpenters' Hall is a tourist attraction.

The colonies were ready to unite. **Delegates** from 12 of the 13 colonies (all the colonies except Georgia) met at Carpenters' Hall in Philadelphia, beginning on September 5, 1774. Members included George Washington and Patrick Henry representing Virginia, and John and Samuel Adams from Massachusetts. This was known as the First Continental Congress.

The Continental Congress decided to respectfully state its complaints against King George III and the British Parliament. In this statement, the colonists reminded Parliament and the king that they were still British citizens and deserved all of the same rights and privileges of British citizens living in England.

Parliament responded by passing additional laws. On March 30, 1775, Great Britain passed the New England Restraining Act, adding even more restrictions on the colonists.

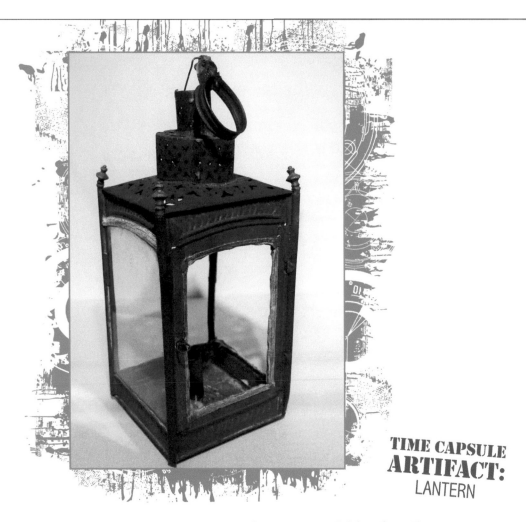

Your next time capsule item could be fragile.
Be careful with the glass as you pull it out to look
at it. This is a lantern that was made famous by a
member of the Sons of Liberty, Paul Revere.

The patriots worried that the British soldiers would find their weapons or arrest them for speaking out against the king. Communicating could be difficult for the rebels. They could only write letters or speak in person. If they wanted to pass along messages or communicate danger, they needed a plan.

Paul Revere came up with the answer. Hundreds of British soldiers were stationed in Boston. The patriots were hiding weapons in the nearby village of Concord. Revere instructed men on the mainland to watch the church tower every night.

If the Redcoats marched off on the only road connecting Boston to the mainland, Revere's men would hang one lit lantern in the steeple of the Old North Church. If the British Army took the shortcut by rowing boats to the shore, they would hang two lit lanterns.

On the night of April 18, 1775, hundreds of British troops had been ordered to Concord to look for weapons. Two lanterns hung in the Old North Church steeple for only 60 seconds, but it was long enough. Paul Revere and others rode ahead to alert John Hancock and Samuel Adams that the British soldiers were on their way.

Contrary to the long-standing legend, Paul Revere did not yell "The British are coming!" as he rode.

Fact

When the British troops arrived in Concord, the **militiamen** were armed and waiting. A gun was fired and shooting began. Eight colonists were killed and nine were wounded. The Revolutionary War had officially begun.

CHAPTER 4

THE REVOLUTIONARY WAR

TIME CAPSULE
ARTIFACT:
GRAND UNION FLAG

In the time capsule, underneath the lantern might be a folded piece of red, white, and blue fabric. It's a flag, but it's not one that is easy to recognize. This flag is called the Grand Union Flag, or the Continental Flag.

Flags are an important symbol of unity. On the verge of war, the colonists needed a flag to represent their military and who they were becoming. Their new flag used the red, white, and blue British flag to acknowledge their connection to Great Britain. But the 13 stripes were added to represent the colonies. This flag shows that the patriots were beginning to separate from Great Britain.

Fact

The Second Continental Congress met in May 1775. It formed the Continental Army and named George Washington as its commander. The colonists were about to go to war.

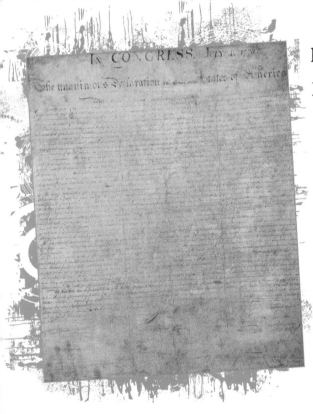

If you pull out a large piece of yellowed **parchment**, be very careful because it is old and fragile. You could be touching one of the most important documents of the United States.

On July 2, 1776, the Second Continental Congress voted to adopt the Declaration of Independence. A printed copy of the Declaration of Independence was sent to Great Britain. It explained the reasons the 13 colonies wanted to become their own country. But Great Britain was not ready to let them go so easily.

Famed Painting

Before photographs were invented, artists often created paintings to honor important events. On Christmas Day in 1776, George Washington crossed the Delaware River, surprising British troops in New Jersey. One of the most famous paintings at the Metropolitan Museum of Art, in New York City, shows this moment in history. It was painted by Emanuel Leutze in 1851.

TIME CAPSULE
ARTIFACT:
COIN

Peering into the time capsule again, something the size of a large button might catch your eye. Reaching for it, your hand feels something metal and cold and you fish it out. It is an old coin.

One of the many problems the colonists faced was money. The United States wasn't a country yet. No one had established banks. But they tried to start a **currency**. Some of the first coins were designed by Benjamin Franklin. Paper money was printed too, but the bills were worthless because there was no central bank system to decide how much of it to make.

The Continental Congress also did not have the ability to raise money or set taxes. Its only option was to depend on donations. The Second Continental Congress decided to seek help from France. France agreed to send the patriots money.

Under Washington's command, the Continental Army fought against the British. A turning point came in October 1777. The American victory during the Second Battle of Saratoga encouraged France to declare war on Great Britain too.

On October 19, 1781, British General Charles Cornwallis surrendered his entire army of Redcoats.

The end of the last major battle of the Revolutionary War is remembered in artist John Trumbull's painting, *Surrender of Lord Cornwallis*. It is on display in the U.S. Capitol building.

The Revolutionary War

- About 133,000 British troops fought

- 56,000 were military soldiers

- 30,000 were German (Hessian) soldiers

- About 96,000 American soldiers fought

- About 35,000 were career soldiers

- About 45,000 were men who joined just to help their country

- About 12,000 French troops fought along with the Americans

- Up to 25,000 formerly enslaved people fought on both sides

- Four of the six Iroquois nations fought alongside the British soldiers (the Mohawk, Cayuga, Onondaga, and the Seneca), while the other two nations (the Oneida and the Tuscarora) fought with the Americans

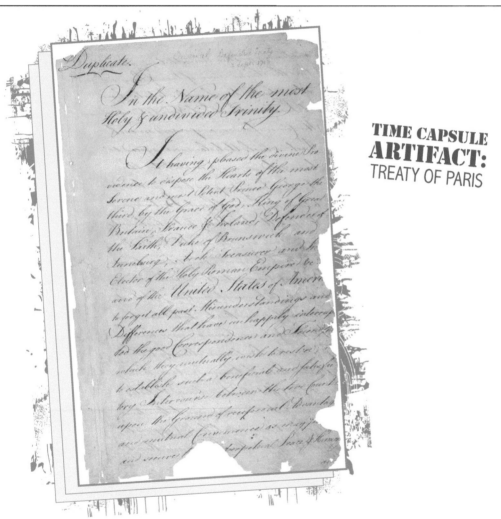

The next item you have in our time capsule could be another important document. Pulling it out, it might be very difficult to read the handwritten words with fancy writing. This document is the Treaty of Paris.

The U.S. and Great Britain negotiated for about a year before the Treaty of Paris was signed.

The Treaty of Paris was signed on September 3, 1783, in Paris, France. It made the end of the war official. It also gave the colonists their independence from Great Britain. The colonists had earned the right and responsibility to establish a new country.

The next item you might find in our time capsule is very large and very heavy. Made of bronze, it weighs 2,080 pounds (943 kilograms). This artifact is the Liberty Bell.

The Liberty Bell was ordered in 1751 by the Pennsylvania Assembly to celebrate its 50th year as a colony. It hung in the tower at the Pennsylvania State House, which is now known as Independence Hall. Any time there was news or announcements, the bell would ring to summon the townspeople. It became an important symbol of freedom and independence.

Today, the Liberty Bell is visible from the street at the Liberty Bell Center. Every Fourth of July, children who are descendants of the signers of the Declaration of Independence gently tap the bell 13 times to honor this important day.

Fact

There is a lot of disagreement about when the bell rang and what caused the cracks. But experts agree that the last time the Liberty Bell was officially rung was to honor George Washington's birthday in 1846.

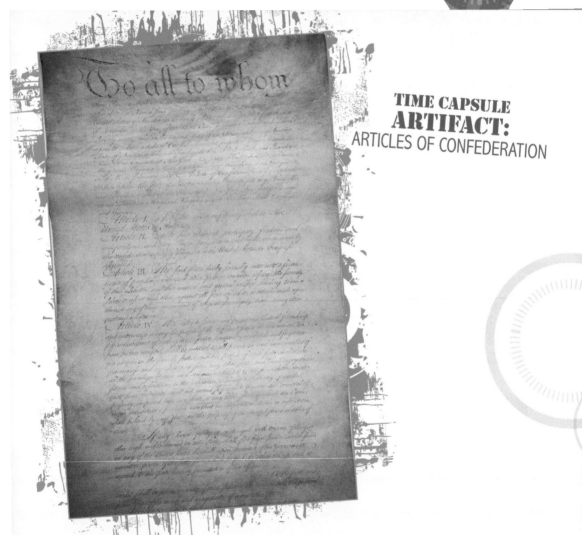

TIME CAPSULE
ARTIFACT:
ARTICLES OF CONFEDERATION

Reaching into the time capsule, you might pull out another stack of old, official-looking papers. This is the Articles of Confederation. These papers established 13 **sovereign** states and set forth the first plan for a government of the new country. Drafted in 1777, they were adopted in 1781.

However, there were problems. The states had their independence and a lot of power. But the national government was weak. The national government also did not have the power to tax the people. It could only ask the states for money.

Before the war was over, the Second Continental Congress worked to create a whole new government. Its first step in creating a new government was to draft the Articles of Confederation.

TIME CAPSULE
ARTIFACT:
FIRST U.S. FLAG

Underneath the set of papers, you can see
that there is another folded piece of old, worn
fabric. When you shake it out, you can see that it
is another flag.

A country's flag is symbolic and important. On June 14, 1777, the Second Continental Congress voted that the flag of the United States should include 13 red and white stripes and 13 stars to represent the 13 original colonies, now called states. It serves as a symbol of strength and unity.

Legend has it that Betsy Ross sewed the first American flag, but there is no evidence that this really happened.

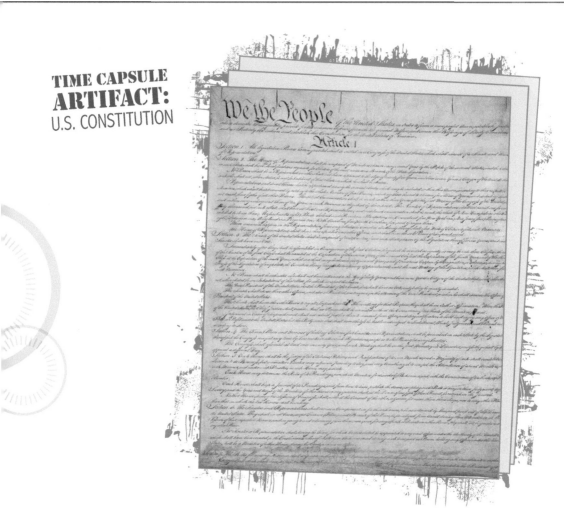

Two more documents might show up in your time capsule, and both are quite important. The first is the Constitution of the United States.

Scene at the Signing of the Constitution of the United States, a 1940 painting by Howard Chandler Christy, hangs in the U.S. Capitol.

On May 25, 1787, delegates from all the states except Rhode Island met again to revise the Articles of Confederation. They ended up writing a new plan altogether.

The delegates agreed that there needed to be central leadership, but there also had to be a separation of powers. They created three different branches of government: the legislative branch, the executive branch, and the judicial branch.

The legislative branch, Congress, makes the laws and is divided into two groups—the Senate and the House of Representatives. The executive branch is led by the president of the United States. The judicial branch consists of courts and judges. They interpret the laws passed by Congress.

On September 15, 1787, the 39 delegates voted to approve and accept the Constitution. The next step was to take it to the state governments for approval. For the Constitution to be adopted, nine of the 13 states had to agree. On December 7, 1787, Delaware, the first state, approved the Constitution. On June 21, 1788, New Hampshire became the ninth state to approve it.

The last document you might find in our time capsule has a large, clear title written across the top: Congress of the United States. It is the Bill of Rights.

While nine states agreed to adopt the Constitution, they also asked for more to be added to it. They wanted a greater guarantee that the rights of the people would be protected.

The Bill of Rights added 10 amendments to the Constitution. The Declaration of Independence, the Constitution, and the Bill of Rights together are considered the three most important founding documents of the United States. Together, they are known as the Charters of Freedom.

Today's lawmakers meet in the U.S. Capitol in Washington, D.C.

The Bill of Rights was approved on December 15, 1791. The document declares that citizens will be guaranteed the right to choose their own religion, the right to speak out freely (even if it's against the government), and the right to a fair trial if a person is accused of a crime.

When the representatives from 12 of the 13 colonies met for the First Continental Congress, they never could have known the path that would follow. They only wanted to be heard by their government. This led the colonists to a bloody war, and they had to fight hard to gain their independence. But ultimately, they won their freedom and established a government that still serves as a successful example of **democracy**.

More About the Artifacts

Redcoat

In the days of the Revolutionary War, most of the British soldiers were professional military men. Their uniforms often reflected their rank. A higher rank in the military meant more decorations on their uniforms.

Handbill About the Tea Act of 1773

On December 2, 1773, Boston patriots passed around these advertisements warning people not to purchase any tea from the shipments that were arriving from the East India Tea Company. They reminded people that everyone voted to boycott tea from Great Britain.

Musket from the Revolutionary War

This is an American militia musket from c. 1760–1777. It is 63 inches (160 centimeters) long and weighs 8.6 pounds (3.9 kilograms). This musket is from the George C. Neumann Collection at Valley Forge National Historical Park in Pennsylvania.

East India Company Tea Chest

This tea chest, found by 15-year-old John Robinson the day after the Boston Tea Party, is one of only two known tea chests to survive the Tea Party.

Petition of the Continental Congress

The scrolled writing across the top of this document reads "To the Kings Most Excellent Majesty" and addresses King George III as "Most Gracious Sovereign." It is part of the Papers of Benjamin Franklin housed at the Library of Congress in Washington, D.C.

Lantern from Old North Church

This was one of the two lanterns that were hung for Paul Revere in the steeple of the Old North Church in Boston. Founded in 1723, the Old North Church is now a historic site and the oldest church in Boston that is still standing.

Grand Union Flag

The Grand Union Flag was the first flag designed for the Continental Army. It was raised for the first time on December 2, 1775, by Lieutenant John Paul Jones on the USS *Alfred*, a warship of the Continental Navy.

Declaration of Independence

The Declaration of Independence is on display at the National Archives Museum in Washington, D.C. Congress approved the final text of the Declaration on July 4, 1776.

Continental Coin

This copper coin was the first to be issued by what became the new nation, the United States, in 1787. Benjamin Franklin is believed to have helped with its design.

Treaty of Paris

This treaty officially ended the Revolutionary War between the American colonies and Great Britain. It is stored at the National Archives Museum.

Liberty Bell

This famous symbol of freedom was originally known as the State House Bell. It used to hang in the bell tower of the Pennsylvania State House (now renamed Independence Hall).

Articles of Confederation

The Articles of Confederation is made out of six pages of parchment, stitched together, and was signed by 48 representatives from 13 states. The document is housed at the National Archives Museum.

First Official American Flag

On June 14, 1777, the Second Continental Congress passed the first Flag Act, declaring "that the Flag of the thirteen United States shall be thirteen stripes, alternate red and white; that the Union be thirteen stars, white on a blue field, representing a new constellation." Flag Day is celebrated on June 14 each year.

Constitution of the United States

The Constitution of the United States originally included seven articles and has been amended 27 times. It is on display at the National Archives Museum.

Bill of Rights

The Bill of Rights contains the first 10 amendments to the Constitution of the United States. The Declaration of Independence, the Constitution of the United States, and the Bill of Rights are known together as the Charters of Freedom. They are displayed together at the National Archives Museum because they are the documents that were instrumental in founding the United States.

Glossary

boycott (BOI-kot)—choose not to purchase a good or service from someone as a form of protest

colonize (KOL-uh-nahz)—to settle among and exert political control over another group of people

currency (KUR-uhn-see)—a system of money for use in a particular country

delegate (DEL-i-git)—a representative authorized to make decisions on behalf of a group of people

democracy (di-MAH-kruh-see)—a form of government in which the citizens can choose their leaders.

extremist (ik-STREE-mist)—a person who holds extreme views and/or resorts to extreme action to promote them

handbill (HAND-bil)—a single piece of paper with a message on it

loyalist (LOI-uh-list)—a person who remains loyal to the established ruler, especially during a time of revolt

militiamen (mi-LISH-uh-men)—a group of citizens fighting together as an army

parchment (PARCH-muhnt)—writing material made from the skin of sheep or goats

patriot (PAY-tree-uht)—a person devoted to defending his or her country of origin

port (PORT)—a place where boats and ships can dock or anchor safely

sovereign (SOV-er-in)—possessing or holding extreme power

treaty (TREE-tee)—an agreement between countries

Read More

Demuth, Patricia Brennan. *What Is the Constitution?*
New York: Penguin Workshop, 2018.

MacCarald, Clara. *The American Revolution.* Lake Elmo, MN:
Focus Readers, 2018.

*Our Nation's Documents: The Written Words that Shaped Our
Country. Time* for Kids. New York: Liberty Street, 2018.

Internet Sites

The Constitution for Kids
https://usconstitution.net/constkids4.html

The Founding Fathers: What Were They Really Like?
https://www.biography.com/news/founding-fathers-
quotes-facts

The Revolutionary War
https://www.americanhistoryforkids.com/the-
revolutionary-war/

Index